COMMITTED
TO HINDUISM

A HINDU COMMUNITY

SYLVIA AND BARRY
SUTCLIFFE

RMEP

RELIGIOUS AND MORAL EDUCATION PRESS

Religious and Moral Education Press
An imprint of Chansitor Publications Ltd,
a wholly owned subsidiary of Hymns Ancient & Modern Ltd
St Mary's Works, St Mary's Plain
Norwich, Norfolk NR3 3BH

First published 1994

ISBN 1-85175-022-3

Acknowledgements
The Authors and Publisher would like to thank the
Management Committee and members of the Shree Sanatan
Mandir, Leicester, particularly those whose interviews appear in
this book, for their generous help. We are especially indebted to
Dipti Mistry, Illa Popat and Ramesh Bakrania for their kind
assistance as our principal contacts at the Mandir.

We are also grateful to Daler Singh for his assistance with the
cover photography and to Exsports, Exeter, for the loan of several
items used in photography.

Designed and typeset by Topics Visual Information, Exeter

Photography by Michael Burton-Pye

Printed in Singapore by Tien Wah Press for
Chansitor Publications Ltd, Norwich

CONTENTS

INTRODUCTION

The books in this **Faith and Commitment** series give you the chance to look at religions and religious denominations (groups within religions) through the personal reflections of people with a religious commitment.

To create these books, we visited local religious communities in different parts of Britain. We talked to people across the range of ages and roles you'd expect to find in a community – parent, child, grandparent, priest, community worker. That is, we interviewed people like you and your family, your friends, the people where you live. We asked them all the same questions and we've used the themes of those questions as chapter headings in the books.

Each chapter contains extracts from those interviews. People interpret our questions as they want to. They talk freely in their own words about religious ideas and personal experiences, putting emphasis where they think it belongs for them. The result is a set of very individual insights into what religion means to some of the people who practise it. A lot of the insights are spiritual ones, so you may have had similar thoughts and experiences yourself, whether or not you consider yourself a 'religious' person.

You will see that some pages include FACT-FINDER boxes. These are linked to what people say in the interview extracts on these pages. They give you bits of back-up information, such as a definition or where to look up a reference to a prayer or a piece of scripture. Remember that these books are not textbooks. We expect you to do some research of your own when you need to. There are plenty of sources to go to and your teacher will be able to help.

There are also photographs all through the books. Many of the items you can see in this book have religious or cultural significance. Some belong to the people whose interview extracts appear on those pages. They are very special to the people who lent them for particular but different reasons, like special things belonging to you.

Committed to Hinduism: A Hindu Community introduces you to eleven Hindus who go to the Shree Sanatan Mandir, the Temple of the Eternal God, in Leicester. In India, Hindu temples tend to be dedicated to specific gods and goddesses. In Britain, because there are fewer of them, Hindu temples cater for a wider range of Hindu belief, usually with shrines to Vishnu, Shiva and the Mother Goddess, as here at the Shree Sanatan Mandir.

SYLVIA AND BARRY SUTCLIFFE

ABOUT ME

 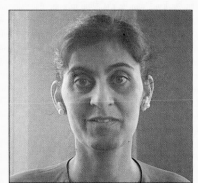 

NAME: *Deena*

WHAT I DO: *I'm in Year 8 at Soar Valley Community College. I'm doing quite well at school.*

MY FAMILY: *I'm thirteen. I've got one brother, a little brother. He's ten.*

MY ROLE IN THE RELIGIOUS COMMUNITY: *I've been coming to the mandir for about seven years. Every Sunday at the mandir we have a Sunday school. There are groups for different ages up to twelve. If a festival's coming up, it's explained to you. Why we celebrate it. What it's for.*

SOME OF MY SPECIAL INTERESTS: *I like painting and listening to music – especially Asian music. I like some kinds of pop music.*

NAME: *Illa*

MY FAMILY: *I was born in India and grew up there in a Hindu family. I got married and came to the U.K. with my husband in 1989. I've got a daughter, Anjani, who's nearly five now. You know about Hanumanji, I expect. Hanumanji's mother's name was Anjani. I've always liked that name.*

MY ROLE IN THE RELIGIOUS COMMUNITY: *I was at home with Anjani for the first two years. I didn't work. Now I work here at the temple and I also teach Gujarati.*

While I was studying for my degree in India, I used to give tuition to children of primary-school age, encouraging them in their language and cultural traditions. That's when I started really being interested in this sort of work.

SOME OF MY SPECIAL INTERESTS: *Cooking, reading – especially the Ramayana and the Bhagavad Gita – Hindi music and Hindi films. I also like playing with my daughter and taking her swimming.*

FACT-FINDER

Hanumanji
Lord Hanuman, the monkey god who used his strength and cleverness to help Rama rescue his wife Sita from the demon-king Ravana. The ending '-ji' is a term of respect meaning 'great'.

Gujarati
Language spoken by people from the state of Gujarat in north-west India.

Ramayana • Bhagavad Gita
Two of the main Hindu sacred books. (See also pages 47 and 39.)

Hindi
One of the languages spoken across India.

NAME: *Ramesh B*

WHAT I DO: *I was born in Nairobi, Kenya. My primary education was in Nairobi, secondary in Mombasa. Those seven years in Mombasa were absolutely great. I have unforgettable memories.*

I came to England with just O-levels. I started work in a laboratory and did physics, chemistry and maths A-levels at evening class — a lot of hard work. I then went to University College, Swansea, and on to Birmingham University to do postgraduate studies. I'm a qualified process engineer.

I'm also a governor of a local community college.

MY FAMILY: *I've got two children. Neera, my daughter, is twenty-one, and Shivit, my son, is nearly fifteen.*

MY ROLE IN THE RELIGIOUS COMMUNITY: *I'm Secretary of the Shree Sanatan Mandir.*

SOME OF MY SPECIAL INTERESTS: *I go jogging regularly. I like doing a bit of carpentry — and cooking. My chapattis are famous!*

MORE ABOUT MY FAMILY

My wife's Niru, my daughter's Neera. It's a bit confusing, but it's all my sister's fault!

Usually, the dad's sister or the mum's brother gives a name to a new child. When the child is born, we look up what we call their rashi for their initial. You look up the stars, all that's mathematically involved, and you get two or three letters from which you can start a name.

We found out that my daughter's name should start with an 'N'. What my sister did was to combine the 'N' with the 'ra' which starts my name. That gave us 'Neera'.

FACT-FINDER

Rashi
Horoscope, a chart showing the positions of the stars and planets when the child was born.

SCHOOL GOVERNORS: A GUIDE TO THE LAW

COUNTY AND CONT... SCHOOLS

ABOUT ME

NAME: *Niru B*	

WHAT I DO: *I came from Mombasa, Kenya, and now live in Leicester. I'm a receptionist in a doctors' surgery.*

MY FAMILY: *I've got two children, a girl and a boy. One is twenty-one, the other will soon be fifteen.*

SOME OF MY SPECIAL INTERESTS: *I play badminton now and then, go to aerobics. I enjoy swimming.*

NAME: *Ashok*

WHAT I DO: *I'm the pujari, the priest, here at the Shree Sanatan Mandir in Leicester.*

MORE ABOUT ME

I came to Britain three years ago from India. All my childhood was spent in India, in the Gujarat city of Baroda. It's where I received my education. I have a BA in Sanskrit and English, an MA in Sanskrit and a BEd in Sanskrit and English. After qualifying, I worked as a secondary high-school teacher in India, teaching Sanskrit.

My father did twenty-four years' service with Indian Railways then took early retirement and went as a religious teacher to Dar es Salaam in Tanzania. He worked there for twelve years. Now he's the priest at the Hindu temple in Southampton.

This is how I came to Britain. My mother was very ill with a lung problem. The outlook wasn't good, and my mother and father wanted to have one of their sons here. There's a religious reason for that. According to Hindu custom, death rituals are performed by either the eldest or the youngest son. My parents were alone, and I'm their youngest son. So I decided to come to Britain if I could. I was fortunate. I applied for and got the job of priest at a Hindu temple in Birmingham.

The contract in Birmingham was for two years. After that, I came to this job in Leicester. The Shree Sanatan Mandir is very big, very busy and very well known. It's one of the oldest in the U.K.

My gift from God is that I'm always happy. I can chat to people who come to the temple, ask them if they have any problems. I can't remove their problems, but I can help them with religious advice.

FACT-FINDER

Sanskrit
Ancient language in which the main Hindu sacred books are written.

NAME: *Ramanbhai*
WHAT I DO: *I work for the Social Services Department in Leicester, but I spend a lot of my time here at the temple.*
MY FAMILY: *I'm married. My wife and I have four children. We also have my elderly mother living with us.*

MY ROLE IN THE RELIGIOUS COMMUNITY

I'm President of the Shree Sanatan Mandir, which is one of the largest Hindu temples in the U.K. During our recent Divali celebrations, we had five thousand visitors, for instance. People were queueing outside in the rain. We're also the headquarters of the National Council of Hindu Temples.

When I first came to Britain in 1964, I joined one of the organizations that teaches the Gujarati language. Gujarati is our mother tongue, and we've done a lot to develop Hinduism in Leicester through work in the mother tongue.

I also belong to the Gujarati Hindu Association. My main interests are in promoting awareness of our culture and helping to provide more cultural programmes for our children.

FACT-FINDER

Divali
Festival of Lights. (See also pages 26–29.)

Gujarati · Mother tongue
Ramanbhai means the Indian language the families spoke before they came to Britain, and may still use today. Many Hindu families in Leicester trace their ancestry back to Gujarat, a state in north-west India. Some moved straight from Gujarat to Britain but many have lived and even been born in places outside India, like East Africa. Here, Gujarati would have been spoken alongside other languages, which is how a strong sense of Gujarati identity, even amongst people who have never been to Gujarat, has been kept alive. People like Ramanbhai are keen to keep that identity going.

NAME: *Dipti*

WHAT I DO: *I was brought up in India and came to this country in 1989. I've got two degrees, one in chemistry and the other in librarianship.*

At the moment, I have three jobs. Two of them involve social work. One is with the Gujarati Hindu Association, which is an umbrella organization for all the Hindu associations in Leicestershire. Then, every evening, I work with the community at Shree Sanatan Temple. I also work for an estate agent.

SOME OF MY SPECIAL INTERESTS: *I enjoy cooking different vegetarian dishes and sewing. I also like reading, walking, watching films and listening to Hindi and Gujarati music.*

MY ROLE IN THE RELIGIOUS COMMUNITY

I've seen the situation of our people in this country and clearly there are needs. I thought, if I could take on community work, it would help meet some of those needs from a cultural, educational and religious point of view. So I started doing community work at the temple.

I've also tried to develop Gujarati education and in 1991 we managed to set up Gujarati classes. Most young children in our families do learn Gujarati at home before they start going to school or nursery. They do understand basic Gujarati conversation at home, but they're poor in writing and reading. There's a situation now, though, where even some of the parents don't know Gujarati. But people are beginning to learn from that experience. So we have kids *and* parents, both, coming to Gujarati classes.

At the moment, we're running seven classes plus one adult class. We're hoping to set up more next year. Also, every Sunday we have a sort of Sunday school for the kids, which helps with their religious education.

FACT-FINDER

Gujarati
From the state of Gujarat in north-west India. Also the language spoken by people from Gujarat.

Hindi
One of the languages spoken across India.

NAME: *Chhotabhaim, but people usually call me by my initials: 'CM'.*

WHAT I DO: *In India, I finished my primary education then went to Dadabhai Navaroji High School in Anand. Mr Dadabhai Navaroji was a Parsee, a very learned man. Later in his life he came to Britain and became the first Indian to sit as an M.P. at Westminster. I'm very proud of that.*

After secondary education, I went to college and finished my BSc degree. I'm a science graduate of Bombay University. After graduating, I worked in India and in Africa as a teacher, first in a primary school, then in a secondary school teaching maths and science. I also did some social work in East Africa.

SOME OF MY SPECIAL INTERESTS: *I enjoy reading. I also spend a lot of my time doing social work and am involved in a support group for mentally handicapped people.*

FACT-FINDER

Parsee
Member of a religious community found mainly in Gujarat and Bombay in India. Parsees are Zoroastrians who trace their ancestry back to Iran, the other main centre where Zoroastrianism is practised today. ('Parsee' means 'Persian'.)

Zoroastrianism is an ancient religion named after its founder Zarathustra. It is quite different to religions like Hinduism and Islam which exist around it. The main feature of Parsee worship is the fire temple, where a fire is kept burning continuously.

NAME: *Dhanlaxmi P*

MY ROLE IN THE RELIGIOUS COMMUNITY: *My husband and I are Brahmin by caste. There are four Brahmins in this community: two priests and us. Being Brahmin gives us special responsibilities. For example, I have to prepare food – symbolic food – for the gods. When it's ready, the priest comes, says prayers over it and takes it to the gods in the temple.*

NAME: *Narnarayam P*

MY FAMILY: *My wife and I were born in Kenya. We came to Leicester in 1969.*

We got married in March 1960. We were introduced by our parents. We sat together, whether we liked it or not. We talked together.

Arranged marriages are happy because surrounding them is a lot of family support. Parents on the groom's side and parents on the bride's side have given the match careful thought. Everyone wants it to succeed.

Recently, I arranged the marriage of my first son.

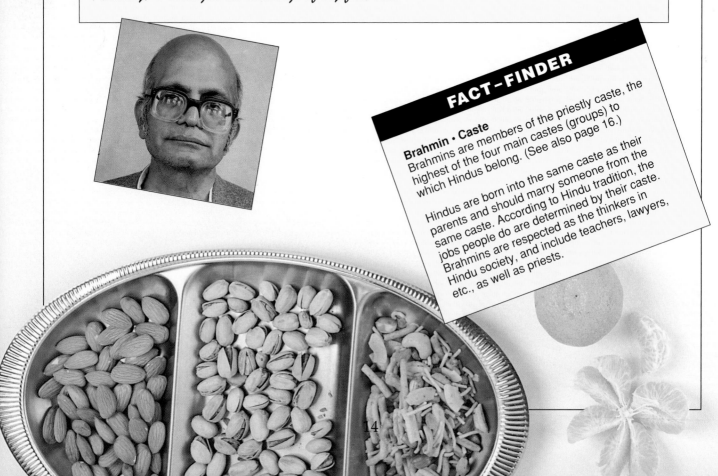

FACT–FINDER

Brahmin • Caste

Brahmins are members of the priestly caste, the highest of the four main castes (groups) to which Hindus belong. (See also page 16.)

Hindus are born into the same caste as their parents and should marry someone from the same caste. According to Hindu tradition, the jobs people do are determined by their caste. Brahmins are respected as the thinkers in Hindu society, and include teachers, lawyers, etc., as well as priests.

NAME: *Prabhulal*

WHAT I DO: *I was born in 1910 in a small village in India. In 1930, I went to Nairobi in East Africa and stayed there as a businessman for thirty-nine years, right up to 1969. Then in 1969, I came to Leicester. Now I'm retired.*

MY ROLE IN THE RELIGIOUS COMMUNITY: *When I first came to Leicester, there was no temple and no Hindu societies or organizations. So we got some people together and started the first temple, the Shree Sanatan Mandir. I was Assistant Treasurer for many years. Now I'm eighty-three, I'm happy just to be a Trustee.*

I've also been involved in running a number of organizations connected with the Hindu community. For a time, I was President of the Gujarati Hindu Association, which is the umbrella body for about fifty other groups.

FACT-FINDER

Trustee
Charities and voluntary groups like the Shree Sanatan Mandir are often run by committees of people elected by other members. They often appoint trustees, who have special responsibility, A trustee may or may not take an active part in on behalf of the group. the day-to-day running of the group.

Gujarati Hindu Association
Association for Hindus whose families come from the state of Gujarat in north-west India.

WHERE
I BELONG

I belong in a Hindu family. It doesn't matter where that family lives, what part of the world. What does matter is that I can call myself a Hindu. That means knowing and understanding the Hindu religion and being able to practise it properly. It means learning more about it and passing what I know on to the next generation. I want the next generation – children like my daughter – to be able to say proudly that they are Hindu.

ILLA

I'm a Brahmin, but more importantly I'm a Hindu. Hindus are divided into so many castes. Even within the Brahmin caste, there are something like eighty-two branches. So my personal idea is that I'm a Hindu. A pure Hindu. That's what matters.

PRABHULAL

FACT-FINDER

Brahmin • Caste
Brahmins are members of the priestly caste, the highest of the four main castes (groups) to which Hindus belong. (See also page 14.)

Note: Hindus also call the four main castes 'varnas' (meaning 'colours') and call the sub-divisions or branches within the varnas 'castes'.

I've got different friends in different places. Most of them are Hindus, but some aren't. Not all of my Hindu friends come here to this temple because they believe in different deities, so they go to other temples. There are different temples and special things go on in them – not always, but sometimes. So my friends get involved in that, but they'll visit other temples as well.

I believe in Ram and Jalaram more because – I don't know. Some of my friends, they believe in Swami Narayan and Radha/Krishna and some of the other deities.

DEENA

First of all, I'm a Hindu. I'm also Gujarati. And I'm British. I came from Kenya originally. In Kenya I felt I was British. When I came here, I felt I was British. I like to call myself a British Hindu.

Hinduism is important to me. It brings a togetherness, an awareness of our culture, that ties families and communities together.

RAMANBHAI

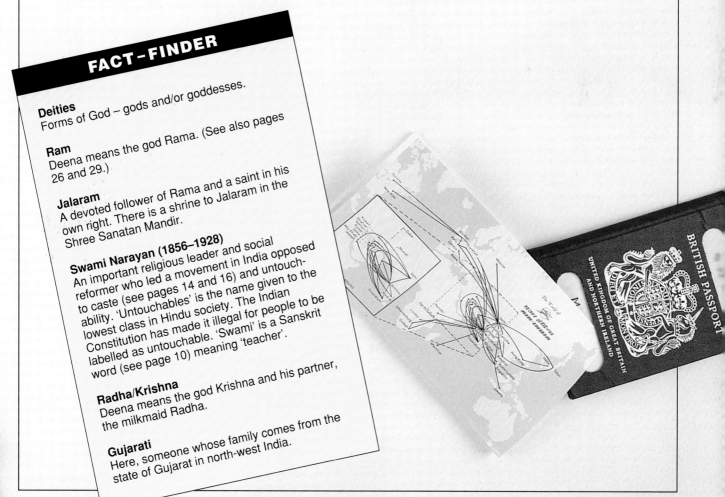

FACT-FINDER

Deities
Forms of God – gods and/or goddesses.

Ram
Deena means the god Rama. (See also pages 26 and 29.)

Jalaram
A devoted follower of Rama and a saint in his own right. There is a shrine to Jalaram in the Shree Sanatan Mandir.

Swami Narayan (1856–1928)
An important religious leader and social reformer who led a movement in India opposed to caste (see pages 14 and 16) and untouch-ability. 'Untouchables' is the name given to the lowest class in Hindu society. The Indian Constitution has made it illegal for people to be labelled as untouchable. 'Swami' is a Sanskrit word (see page 10) meaning 'teacher'.

Radha/Krishna
Deena means the god Krishna and his partner, the milkmaid Radha.

Gujarati
Here, someone whose family comes from the state of Gujarat in north-west India.

R eligion is a very superficial word to me. Dharma is a very important one. It's the basis of my life.

Everything in creation has dharma. Even God has dharma. Dharma is the quality which is special to each and every being that exists, whatever it is. A fire burns, that's its dharma.

Dharma brings protection. It also brings duties and responsibilities. People who observe dharma are protected by it, but they are also expected to protect others by serving and respecting them. That's part of our human dharma. Whether other people believe in dharma or not makes no difference to my duty to show them love and respect. Because what I see is a creation of God, and I should protect it and honour it. Dharma teaches us to maintain a devotional relationship with God and his creation: people, animals, plants, minerals and the whole universe.

It's easy to look at Hinduism and see just the superficial things – the praying in corners, ringing the bell, the flowers, the ritual. Those things are just starting-points. It's like when you first go to school. You have to learn a bit of self-control before you start real learning. Rituals are basic preparation for advanced worship and yoga.

But dharma is what matters. Understanding dharma through study of religious books like the Vedas, which reveal the quality of God and his creation. Following your own dharma while trying to live in harmony with the dharma of others evolves respect, beauty and love.

'CM'

FACT-FINDER

Dharma
Right behaviour, a (right) way of life, duties (particularly religious duties) that should be performed.

Ringing the bell
When Hindus arrive at a shrine, they usually ring a bell in order to attract the attention of the god(s) and/or goddess(es) worshipped there.

Yoga
A Hindu form of meditation. (See also 'Lotus position' definition on page 30.)

Vedas
The oldest group of Hindu sacred books. Literally, 'veda' means 'knowledge'.

WHAT I FEEL STRONGLY ABOUT

Some people think that Hindus are idol worshippers. They see our images of the gods and don't understand that we, like them, worship one God. What's different is that Hinduism has many branches, like a mighty tree. There's beauty in a tree with many branches, but all the branches come back to one trunk, to one God. And all the branches bear the same fruit.

What we're worshipping isn't idols but sets of ideals. Take Lord Rama, for example. Rama teaches about things like family values, respect and obedience, justice in war, democracy. These are important ideals.

Lord Krishna was born in a prison and taken to cowherd foster-parents. He taught the world that, no matter where you're born, you can grow and develop spiritually and you can help other people. These are ideals that are always in our minds.

'CM'

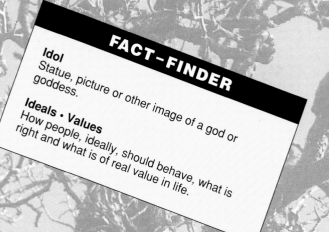

FACT-FINDER

Idol
Statue, picture or other image of a god or goddess.

Ideals • Values
How people, ideally, should behave, what is right and what is of real value in life.

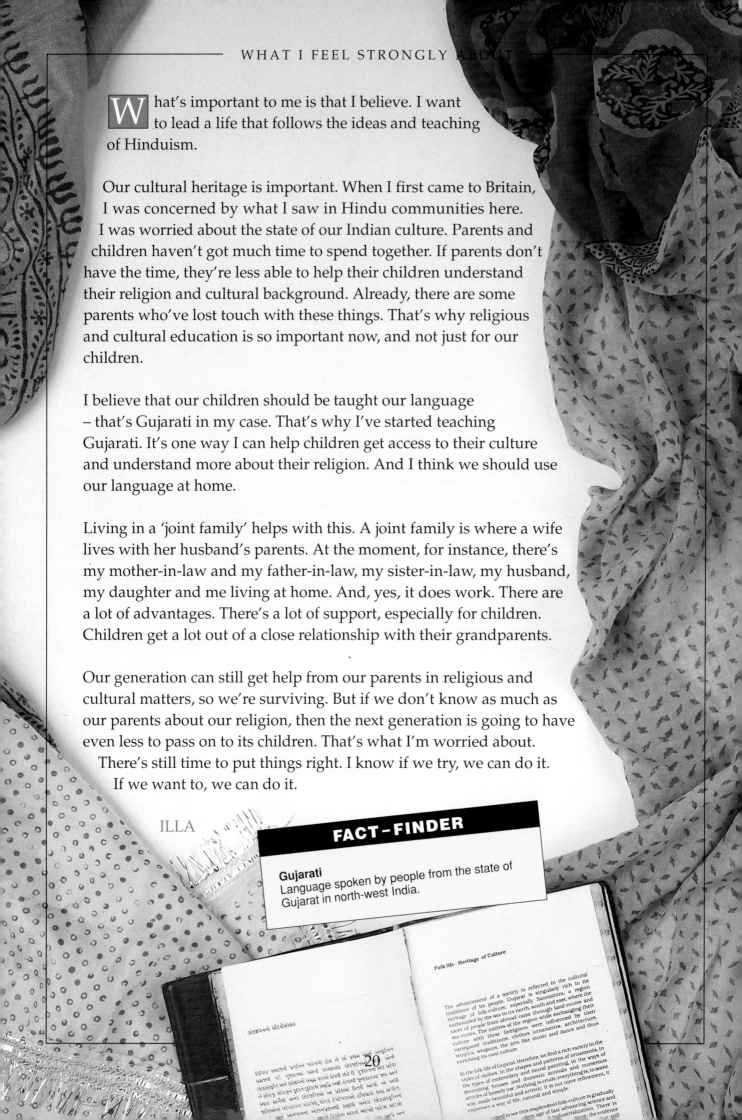

What's important to me is that I believe. I want to lead a life that follows the ideas and teaching of Hinduism.

Our cultural heritage is important. When I first came to Britain, I was concerned by what I saw in Hindu communities here. I was worried about the state of our Indian culture. Parents and children haven't got much time to spend together. If parents don't have the time, they're less able to help their children understand their religion and cultural background. Already, there are some parents who've lost touch with these things. That's why religious and cultural education is so important now, and not just for our children.

I believe that our children should be taught our language – that's Gujarati in my case. That's why I've started teaching Gujarati. It's one way I can help children get access to their culture and understand more about their religion. And I think we should use our language at home.

Living in a 'joint family' helps with this. A joint family is where a wife lives with her husband's parents. At the moment, for instance, there's my mother-in-law and my father-in-law, my sister-in-law, my husband, my daughter and me living at home. And, yes, it does work. There are a lot of advantages. There's a lot of support, especially for children. Children get a lot out of a close relationship with their grandparents.

Our generation can still get help from our parents in religious and cultural matters, so we're surviving. But if we don't know as much as our parents about our religion, then the next generation is going to have even less to pass on to its children. That's what I'm worried about.

There's still time to put things right. I know if we try, we can do it.

If we want to, we can do it.

ILLA

FACT-FINDER

Gujarati
Language spoken by people from the state of Gujarat in north-west India.

20

I don't say anything and I won't do anything until I fully understand it. I take the blessing from the Goddess because I know it is the Goddess. But if my mum or somebody else tells me to do something, I'll ask why first. Because if I don't understand it, I won't want to do it.

Some of my friends, they sort of do things when they don't understand. I say, 'Why do you do it?'

They say, 'Because we have to do it.' I don't like that. I've asked and found out about most of the things I don't understand about Hinduism.

I think Hinduism's just another path to God – to get closer to him – like any other path. If you've been brought up, like me, going up one particular path since you were little then you keep going. I've been going to the temple since I was six. Of course, there's loads of other religions, sometimes similar, sometimes totally different. But they're all just the same, I think – all paths to God.

DEENA

Shiva teaches us that God is with us always in our hearts. When we pray, we must try to pray to God inside us. In human beings, God is on the inside, not the outside. That's a very important idea to me. It's central to what I believe.

NARNARAYAM P

God is one. That's essential. There are a lot of names for God in the world, but there's only one God.

PRABHULAL

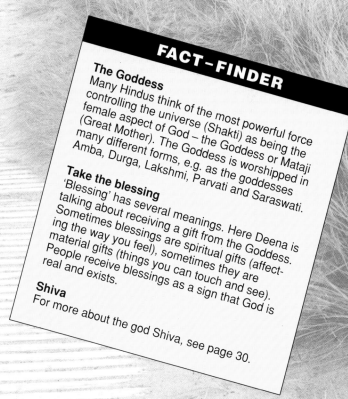

FACT-FINDER

The Goddess
Many Hindus think of the most powerful force controlling the universe (Shakti) as being the female aspect of God – the Goddess or Mataji (Great Mother). The Goddess is worshipped in many different forms, e.g. as the goddesses Amba, Durga, Lakshmi, Parvati and Saraswati.

Take the blessing
'Blessing' has several meanings. Here Deena is talking about receiving a gift from the Goddess. Sometimes blessings are spiritual gifts (affecting the way you feel), sometimes they are material gifts (things you can touch and see). People receive blessings as a sign that God is real and exists.

Shiva
For more about the god Shiva, see page 30.

I feel strongly about several issues facing me and the Hindu religion. First of all, obviously I feel strongly about being in the religion I was born into. But I also feel strongly about all religions because I think at the end of the day there's one God. We may worship God in different ways and emphasize different ideals and ideas. But religion itself is important.

Hinduism is a liberal religion. I wouldn't want to compare it with other religions. That would be insensitive. But we don't go out and convert people. Everybody's welcome.

In Hinduism you worship whatever's important to you. For instance, a tree saves your life, it gives you shade and saves your life. So you take an altar to the tree. That's Hinduism. How you worship depends on what you feel strongly about. You might feel strongly about Shiva or Krishna or Rama or the Mother Goddess Mataji.

Hinduism is about ideals and knowledge. So when you reflect about life, think about things, it directs you positively towards being a better person. That's very important these days, I think.

An issue for this community is bridging the gap between the elderly and the young. I think it's a problem common to all religions, but we have it more acutely because of the communication problem.

For instance, we speak Gujarati, but we can't force our children to learn Gujarati. All right, they learn it at home when they're very young. It's the language their mother talks in. But once they start growing up, with the pressure of college and school, it's very difficult for them to give up the time to learn our language. Then there's a communication barrier.

This is where the rifts start. It's why I'm trying to get youngsters to come into the temple, learn about Hinduism and understand the point of view of older people in our community – how to respect them, things like that. I want more youngsters to come to the temple. Not to be religious fanatics. We don't just discuss religion, we discuss live issues, like arranged marriages, racism, sport.

FACT-FINDER

Liberal
Here, with a broad-minded outlook, without strict rules.

Altar
Here, a flat surface on which offerings to God (e.g. flowers) can be placed.

Shiva • Krishna • Rama
Three of the best-known Hindu gods.

Mataji
Many Hindus think of the most powerful force controlling the universe (Shakti) as being the female aspect of God – the Goddess or Mataji (Great Mother). The Goddess is worshipped in many different forms, e.g. as the goddesses Amba, Durga, Lakshmi, Parvati and Saraswati.

Gujarati
Language spoken by people from the state of Gujarat in north-west India.

For ethnic minorities, there's the racism issue. I've been involved in discrimination at work, racist incidents at work – and that's with a major public-sector employer. We took the matter to the Equal Opportunities Commission and won. It didn't really help me as it turned out, but it's helped other ethnic-minority colleagues.

When something like that happens to you, it's only natural you become more aware of the issues. I've tried to respond positively. For instance, I'm a professional badminton coach. In Leicestershire, there are hardly any coloured players at county level. So I thought, 'OK, now I'm in a position to do something about it, I'll start up some groups.' It looks as if they're successful. And I've started women's groups, too, because I think, as well as ethnic minorities, women are losing out, both in employment and outside. For coloured women particularly, with the culture as it is and the difficulties they face, it's very hard for them to get out.

RAMESH B

One thing I feel strongly about is education. Have you heard of Shankaracharya? He was a brilliant Hindu philosopher and commentator. He said that 'without knowledge there cannot be mukti'. This means without knowledge, God cannot be reached. You can't pray without understanding, for instance.

We need education to understand and fulfil our religion. Some of the people who come to this temple don't know their religion. A lot have been born in Britain. Some haven't had a proper Hindu education. They know the names of the deities – this is Krishna, this is Rama, this is Shiva. But on technical matters or questions of scripture they're stuck.

There's a poem in Sanskrit which translates like this:

With education comes knowledge,
With knowledge comes respect,
With knowledge and respect comes status,
With these come good works and wealth.

Education gives us access to good jobs. Good jobs earn good money. With that money we can do religious work, because money is needed for religious work – it's a materialistic world we live in.
So start by getting education. Later, you'll be in a stronger position to protect your religion.

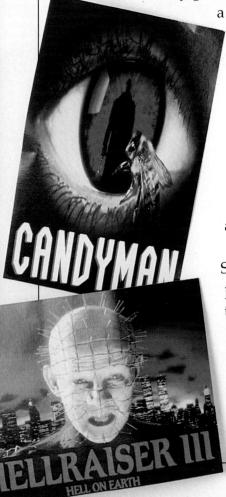

I think one of the problems of the moment in our Hindu community in Britain is that young people are losing the idea of sin. Who can blame them if, for example, they see a violent film and take it as a model?

So I think it's important to provide our youngsters with the chance of a Hindu religious education and other models to follow. It's important to help them understand about

FACT-FINDER

Deities
Forms of God – gods and/or goddesses.

Sanskrit
Ancient language in which the main Hindu sacred books are written.

Idea of sin
Idea that certain ways of behaving are wrong.

Gandhiji
Mohandas K. Gandhi (1869–1948), a Hindu thinker and reformer who led a non-violent protest movement to free India from British rule. The ending '-ji' is a term of respect meaning 'great'.

Shankaracharya (c. 700 C.E.)
One of the most influential religious thinkers in the history of Hinduism. He wrote famous commentaries on three of the main Hindu sacred books: the Vedas, the Upanishads and the Bhagavad Gita.

Swami Vivekananda (1863–1902)
A leading spokesman for modern Hinduism who drew the Western world's attention to Hinduism after his powerful speech at the World's Parliament of Religions in Chicago in 1893. 'Swami' is Sanskrit for 'teacher'.

Vivekananda attracted followers from the West and India. He founded the Ramakrishna Mission in India to help them carry out their work of education and service.

Ramakrishna Paramahansa (1836–1886)
A priest at the temple of the goddess Kali in Daxineshwar near Calcutta who went on to become a 'sanyasin'. This means that, at a special ceremony, he broke all ties with the world and promised to live unmarried, homeless and poor, begging for food and going naked or wearing only a special robe.

Ramakrishna influenced a number of Hindu thinkers of the time. For instance, he was guru (teacher) to Swami Vivekananda.

sin and know what the alternatives are. The Hindu tradition has a lot to offer: good stories – and not just in scripture – and good people, like Gandhiji, Shankaracharya, Swami Vivekananda, Ramakrishna Paramahansa. They're good people with good lessons to give.

ASHOK

Hinduism is a liberal religion. It's profound, of course, but it's not particularly strict, so observing Hinduism isn't difficult.

The two great epics, the Ramayana and the Gita, are our lives. The message of Lord Krishna in the Gita and of Lord Rama in the Ramayana is that we can and should lead good lives. These principles are in us. We're living with them every day, in everything we do.

The Ramayana and the Gita are easy for people to get into. The story of the Ramayana is the story of a family – Rama, his wife Sita, his four brothers, his father. It gives us a model of family life and reinforces the importance of the family. The Gita shows us that we should act truthfully and fight against anything which is evil.

RAMANBHAI

FACT-FINDER

Liberal
Here, with a broad-minded outlook, allowing individuals freedom in how they practise their religion.

Epics
Epics are (very) long narrative poems, i.e. poems that tell stories.

Gita
Literally 'song'. Ramanbhai means the Bhagavad Gita (Song of the Lord), which is part of the Mahabharata, one of the main Hindu sacred books. (See also page 39.)

MY FAVOURITE FESTIVAL

There are so many festivals. There are some which I didn't know a lot about until I became Secretary of the temple. Now I'm learning. That's one of the reasons I come to the temple – to get more knowledge about my religion. In Hinduism you learn, learn, then learn.

Divali and New Year have to be my favourite festivals. As children, we loved it. It's like Christmas.

As kids, you're up at five in the morning. You've put on your best clothes. Mum's done the prayers. Everyone's excited. You go out with your fire-crackers and meet up with your friends. Who's got the biggest cracker? Who's got the best cracker?

The whole house is cleaned in readiness. You put out your best things. People will come round and you'll offer sweets blessed by God. You go to other families' houses. People are very active seeing one another. There are functions going on. You'll probably meet everyone else in the street, whether they're good friends or enemies. If they're enemies, you'll try to make it up.

The background is Rama having defeated Ravana, the demon-king, and coming home.

RAMESH B

FACT-FINDER

New Year
Many Hindus, particularly those from north India, celebrate New Year in October or November, during Divali.

Rama · Ravana
The story of how the god Rama rescued his wife Sita from Ravana is told in the Ramayana, one of the main Hindu sacred books.

Divali is my favourite. It's a very special occasion for all Hindus. It's the occasion of the victory of truth over evil. Also, it's a festival of light, singing, dancing, enjoyment. On Divali night or the following night, New Year's Night, families get together, have a big dinner together and enjoy themselves. Also there are community gatherings. There are a lot of communities within Hinduism, and those communities have their own separate functions.

Divali night is also when Gujarati Hindu businessmen start their new account books. Before they do, they worship Lakshmi, the goddess of wealth, and Ganesha, god of fortune, to help their business in the coming year. It's called Lakshmi Puja.

DIPTI

FACT-FINDER

Gujarati
From the state of Gujarat in north-west India.

Puja
Act of worship during which offerings are made to a god or goddess.

There are a lot of festivals, but generally New Year is the happiest day for me. We always get together – families, friends. We think of the year ahead and the things we could be doing better.

NARNARAYAM P

Festivals are a way of appreciating God and thanking him for what he is and what he's done.

I like Navratri and Divali most. They're big festivals, so people teach you what's going on and go through them with you. Sometimes the festivals are complicated and I don't understand them. When people explain them, it makes it more interesting. The way they celebrate here at this temple is really interesting.

Navratri is about all the goddesses. We put a picture of Mataji in the centre of the temple and all goddesses dance round it. And we dance. We get in a circle and walk round, and clap, and step backwards and forwards. It's like going round and round the Mother Goddess.

There's also the danda ras, the stick dances. We don't usually do them here at the temple because there's not enough space and people get hurt. They do the danda ras in the hall. It's sort of extra.

When Rama returned from the forest after fourteen years, people welcomed him back with lights. That's carried on being done. We do it now, at Divali. We have lots of divas to welcome God with light. We have fireworks, too. That's to go with the divas – more light and celebration.

My mum makes special foods – sweet things. Then people come to our house or we go to other people's houses. We have a little bit of sweet food to celebrate, then we go to the temple.

When I was little, at Divali I used to think of a forest and Rama and Sita and Lakshman walking through it with all these little divas twinkling in the trees and everywhere. I used to think that's what Divali was all about. Then, as I got older, I realized it's to do with the story in the Ramayana and good and evil.

I recently took part in a havan. It was for the thirteen to thirty-one age group. The havan was celebrating the anniversary of when the murti of Mataji first came to the mandir. It was bought in 1976, I think.

A havan's a small fire. Things are put into it, like incense sticks. It's like you're feeding God. Because it was for younger people, the havan was so we could get fire in our education, stay strong and believe in God.

One of the speakers said, 'If you haven't got religion, if you haven't got faith and don't believe in anything, you won't get anywhere.' Quite a lot of people say that.

DEENA

FACT-FINDER

Mataji
Many Hindus think of the most powerful force controlling the universe (Shakti) as being the female aspect of God – the Goddess or Mataji (Great Mother). The Goddess is worshipped in many different forms, e.g. as the goddesses Amba, Durga, Lakshmi, Parvati and Saraswati. The picture Deena mentions shows Mataji in the form of the goddess Durga.

Diva
Small lamp, often made of clay, that burns ghee (melted butter) or oil.

Rama · Sita · Lakshman
When the god Rama had to go into exile for fourteen years, his wife Sita and brother Lakshman went with him. Before they all returned home, the brothers had to rescue Sita from the demon-king Ravana.

Ramayana
Sacred book which tells the story of Rama.

Murti
Image (statue or picture) of a Hindu god or goddess. This murti at the Shree Sanatan Mandir (Temple) is a statue showing Mataji in the form of the goddess Amba.

I enjoy everything, whatever the festival. My favourite festival is Divali. We exchange gifts, make new friends. If you have any quarrels with family or friends, you make it up on that day. You forgive each other for what you've done in the past, go out and enjoy yourself.

NIRU B

All festivals bring happiness, pleasure and enjoyment. That's what a festival should do. It's a time to put work aside, relax the mind, take an interest in life and enjoy it. Because God gave us this life. The world's full of living things, but human beings alone have knowledge, an ability to express ideas, an understanding of good and bad. God gave us life. The festivals are a chance to appreciate it.

In Hinduism, there are two, three or even four festivals in some months. Now, for instance, we're in Sravan. It's the Hindu month which covers parts of July and August. Sravan is the king of the festival months. There are nearly twenty festivals during Sravan. In India, when I was working as a teacher, there'd be only twelve or thirteen school days in the month.

My favourite festival is Shivratri. Shivratri means 'Lord Shiva's night', and Lord Shiva is my favourite deity. He has been since I was a child. I'm a Brahmin, and Brahmins tend to worship Shiva more than the other deities. I go to Shiva's shrine every day.

Lord Shiva is commander-in-chief of the deities. Shiva gives us many moral lessons. Like the other deities, he has a thousand names. But Shiva is different. He is serious, simple living and high thinking. You've seen the pictures of the deities, I expect. Lord Vishnu and Lord Krishna are very attractive deities. Lord Vishnu has ornaments, good clothes, possessions, wealth. But Lord Shiva wears only a lionskin. He's naked – yet he has everything. He has the whole world in his hand. And he likes to give to others. This is his quality.

Lord Shiva is also the controller of the senses. You see him sitting in the lotus position with his eyes closed. Human beings, even priests, are slaves to their senses. Controlling them is hard. But Shiva instructs us to control our senses. That's why Lord Shiva is my favourite deity.

FACT–FINDER

Deities
Forms of God – gods and/or goddesses.

Brahmin
Member of the priestly caste, the highest of the four main castes (groups) to which Hindus belong. (See also pages 14 and 16.)

Lotus position
Basic cross-legged position used in yoga, a Hindu form of meditation. (The 'yoga' practised by non-Hindus often consists of relaxation exercises based on yoga positions.)

Although Shivratri comes every month, people don't celebrate it every month because there are a lot of other deities, too – favourite deities, family deities. But at Shivratri in the Hindu month of Maha, which is around January/February, we have the big festival of Lord Shiva, Mahashivratri, which everyone celebrates.

ASHOK

L ord Shiva is the image that comes to mind when I think of my faith. I always think about Lord Shiva. Brahmin people are particularly attached to Lord Shiva. Women also have a special affection for Shiva. I always pray to Shiva.

It was Lord Shiva who explained the importance of the soul. So we try to concentrate, to go into our souls. The soul is like a light burning within us. In a temple of Shiva you'll find, right in the corner, a light. That's a symbol of the soul.

Shivratri is my favourite festival. That's the special day of our god Shiva. Shivratri's a special occasion for everyone.

DHANLAXMI P

FACT-FINDER

Brahmin
See opposite.

Soul
Innermost part of a person, also called 'atman' by Hindus. The part that Hindus believe survives when the body dies.

I n Hinduism, there are three main festivals. One is Shivratri, Lord Shiva's night. Another is Janamashtami, Lord Krishna's birthday. The third is Ramnavami, that celebrates the birth of Rama. These are big festivals here in Leicester.

I celebrate them all, but I'm a Brahmin, so Shivratri is the most important one to me personally.

PRABHULAL

We have several festivals that celebrate appearances of God. We believe in one God without form. But when there is disorder or a decline in righteousness, the energy of God comes down to protect human beings and the universe. Lord Krishna and Lord Rama are incarnations of God, and their birthdays are celebrated as festivals.

Lord Shiva's spiritual knowledge and power are remembered at Shivratri. Shivratri is a festival I like. It teaches us to move from bad to good, cruelty to compassion, illusion to reality, hatred to love, darkness to light.

Divali and Navratri are also great festivals to me. We enjoy Divali very much because it lasts for four days and we see the New Year coming in. We try to forget any grievances we have. We try to meet friends and relatives, go to the temple, even worship outside in the park or some place where we can enjoy nature. It's a good time, full of prayer and enjoyment. Because these are very holy days, we don't eat any form of meat. Most Hindus are vegetarian anyway, but those that aren't eat vegetarian food at this time.

'CM'

FACT-FINDER

Incarnations
Literally 'forms made of flesh'. Here, appearances in human form.

Navratri
At Navratri, Hindus from Gujarat worship the Mother Goddess, Mataji. (See also page 28.)

Divali · New Year
Many Hindus, particularly those from north India, celebrate New Year in October or November, during Divali, the Festival of Lights. (See also pages 26–29.)

Gita
Literally 'song'. Ramanbhai means the Bhagavad Gita (Song of the Lord), which is part of the Mahabharata, one of the main Hindu sacred books. (See also page 39.)

My favourite festival is Janamashtami, the birthday of Lord Krishna. Most Hindus will fast on that day. We remember Lord Krishna and the stories about him in the Gita. We celebrate his birthday at the temple with devotional songs. We go through the story of how Lord Krishna was born.

RAMANBHAI

ll the festivals have their own interest and their own significance. If you know and understand the festivals in the proper way, they're all important.

But I do have a favourite, and it's Janamashtami. Janamashtami is the birthday of Krishna. He was a supreme power born in a human being. At the time of his birth, there were many demons threatening the country. Krishna brought light. He was a great warrior. He was a great dancer. He was a great musician. That's why I like celebrating Janamashtami.

On Janamashtami, we fast all day, from morning to midnight. When Krishna was born, his parents were in jail. They had nothing. So we try to remember the day by remembering the experience of the parents. If we were faced with their difficulties, could we overcome them? That's what we're asking ourselves when we fast. Some people don't have anything except milk and tea. Others try to eat as little as possible, just potatoes for example.

We pay our respects to Lord Krishna. In Leicester, we celebrate his birth at half past seven in the evening but in India celebrations take place at midnight, which is when he was born. We go to the temple to pray, and in the temple we make a big occasion of the ceremony of the birth of Krishna. There's a procession, and we have parents who offer to be Krishna's parents, taking the roles. At the moment when Krishna is born, they find a boy who's about a year old, put him in a basket and carry him on their heads in the procession. It's accompanied by singing and dancing and prayers. People are praising God for the birth of Krishna and the benefits he brought to the world.

ILLA

FACT-FINDER

Soul
Innermost part of a person, also called 'atman' by Hindus. The part that Hindus believe survives when the body dies.

A
SPECIAL MOMENT

I t happened when I went with my family to India and visited lots and lots of temples. We went to one temple where there was a holy person. I can't remember where it was, but I can see it in my mind. Loads of people go to this holy woman and there were lots of people in the temple.

She came in and sat down – she'd just been to rest or something. She looked really simple. I thought, 'Holy person? Yeah.'

Lots of ill people go to her. She tells them how to get better. What was really weird was that she knew the names of everyone who sat down with her, and where they came from and everything about them. I don't know how she did it.

As soon as we sat down, she used Dad's name. How can someone tell every single person in the whole wide world who they are and what they are?

Some people act this sort of thing. They con you. But she just knew. I didn't think she'd be able to.

When you see something like that, you really can believe that there is such a thing as God.

DEENA

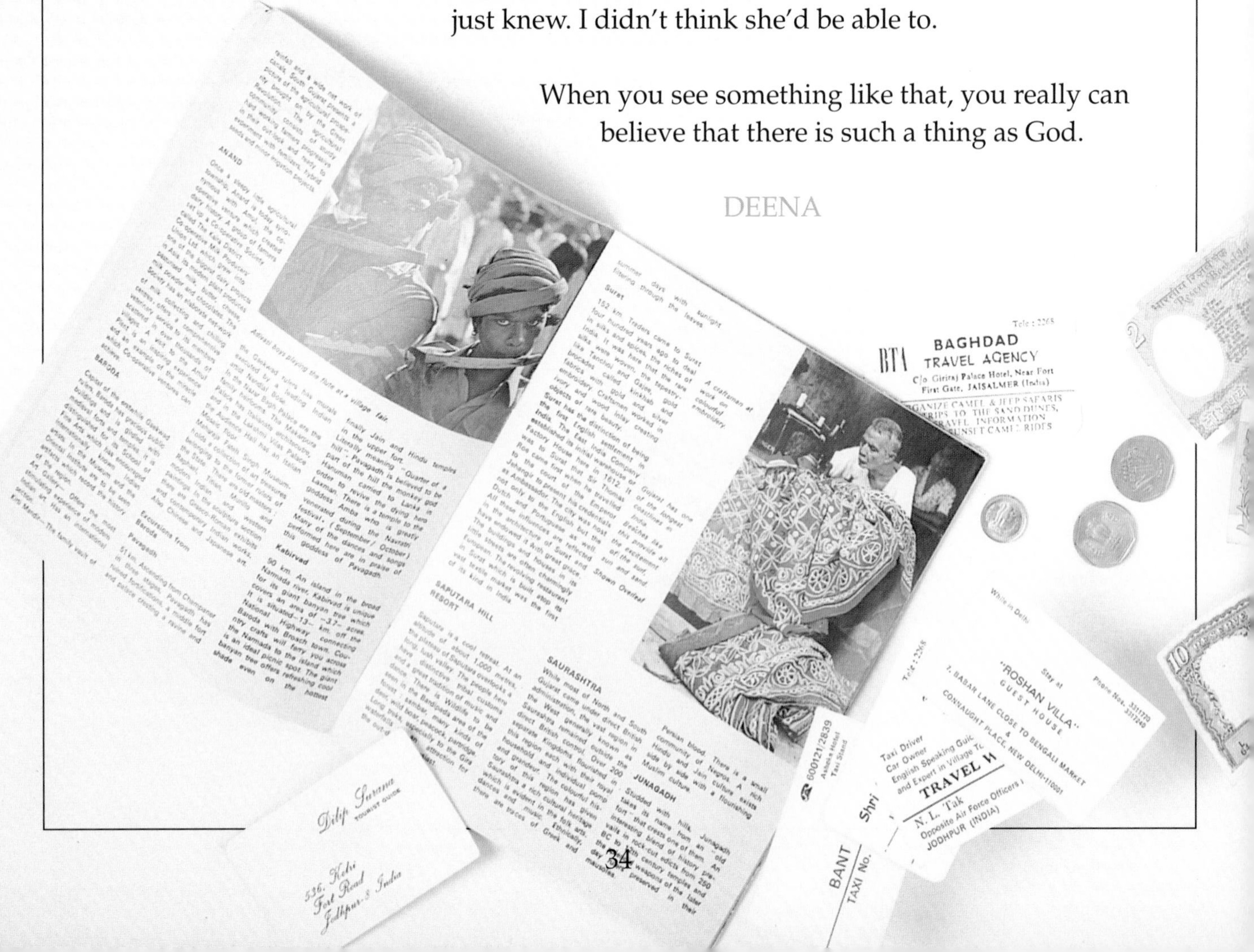

34

S ometimes you don't realize how important something is. When it's there with you, you take it for granted.

I went back to India in 1991 with my husband and daughter. My sister was getting married. For fifteen days, we went on tour, going to all the well-known places. My parents knew we'd be going to visit them after that, but because we were touring we didn't know exactly when we'd reach them.

So I rang from the station when we arrived in my home town. Then we set off for my parents' place. As we got closer, I was praying, 'O God, give me wings so that I can fly to them.' And there they were, waiting in the street for me. I can't explain in words the moment and how joyous it was. My mother was literally crying to see me – you know what mothers are!

I didn't realize until I was there with them how important they are to me. As children, we don't really notice what our parents do for us. Then suddenly you see them for who they are and you recognize what an important role they've had in your life. Especially if – like me – you've been really far away from them.

That was a special moment for me. It's why I just work part-time. I want to devote time to my daughter.

ILLA

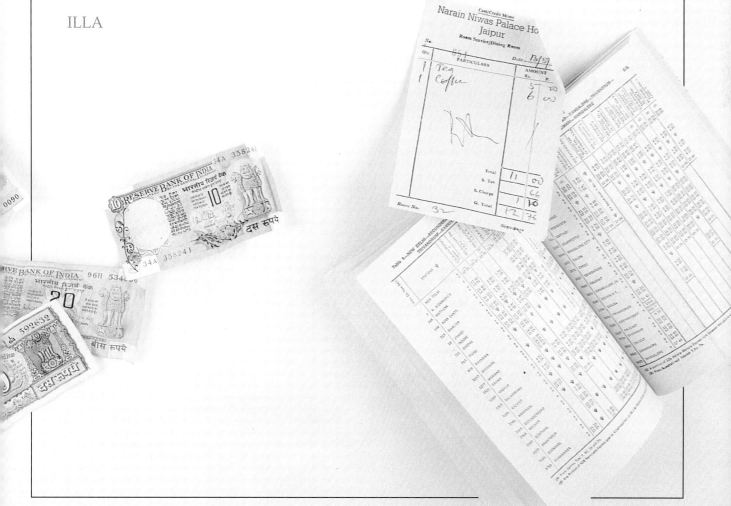

A special moment was when I met my husband. He'd come to India from England. On the eighth of March – I think it was a Thursday – he arrived with his parents at my parents' home in Surat, a city in Gujarat. We served them tea and refreshments. Later I had half-an-hour's talk with him in private, then went out with him for an hour. The following hour we got engaged. All in one day. We were married within a week.

It was a small wedding. Only four hundred guests.

As far as my own experience goes and that of close relatives and friends, arranged marriage does work. In India it's a bit different to here, although things are starting to move with the times in Britain too. There's more time given to letting the couple get to know each other first, accepting that people need time to get to know each other. If both sides are happy with each other, they go further. In the end, the decision's theirs. If they say no, then that's it, full stop, and the families look for another person.

If there is any conflict in marriage, what happens is that the couple try to sort it out with close family members first. If that doesn't work, they go to the community leader and try to sort it out within the community. If the marriage is still going wrong, then they may go to court.

DIPTI

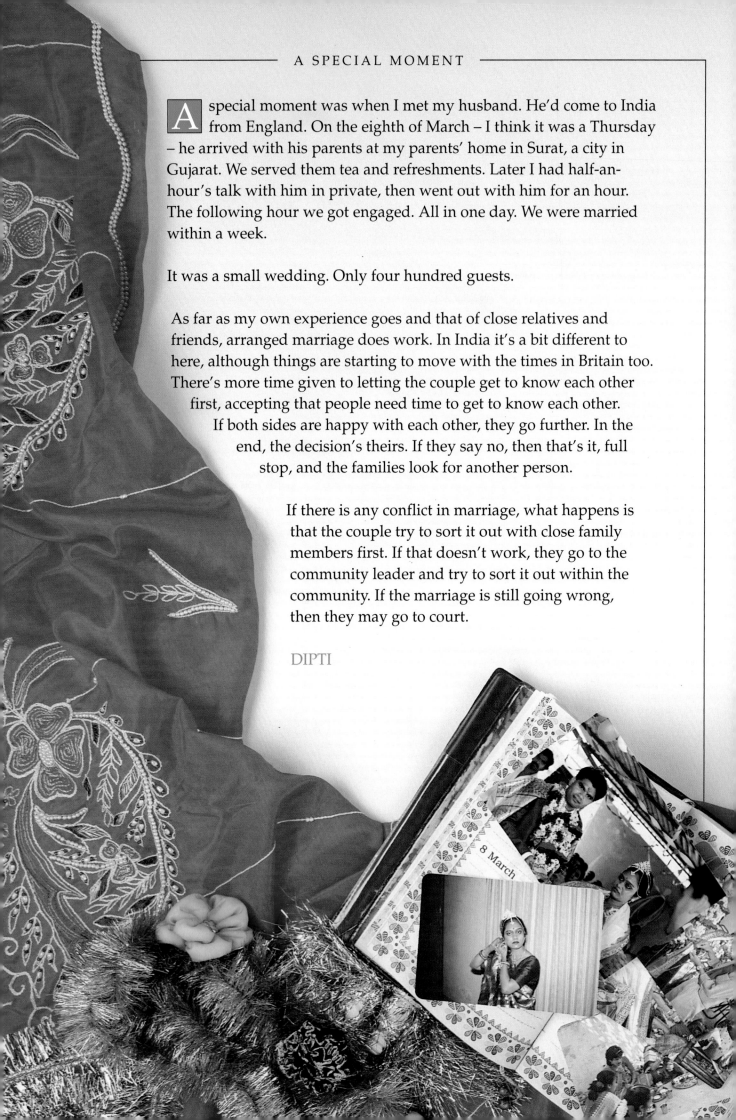

A special moment for me was the birth of my first child. It was knowing she was born into a Hindu family. Knowing she would be growing up to respect the Hindu religion and possibly doing things in the religion.

NIRU B

A special moment – well, actually, it's much more than a single moment – has to be my relationship with my wife. Her family used to visit mine when I lived in Nairobi as a child. I liked her then. We moved to Mombasa when I was ten or eleven – Mombasa's where her family lived – and the relationship just grew. I came to England in my late teens then went back to Kenya to marry her.

It wasn't an arranged marriage, it was a love marriage. Not all Hindu marriages are arranged. It's about fifty-fifty. You have arranged marriages where parents want their children to marry within their community. But in a lot of cases the children, the couple, decide for themselves. Some parents go along with it, some object. That's normal, as in everything.

Both types of marriage tend to work, but we're finding that divorces and difficulties within marriages are slowly increasing. Mainly, that's because of the circumstances and social life around here. There's a lot of pressure.

RAMESH B

M y special moment came during meditation. It was only a couple of seconds, but during those seconds I was somewhere else, somewhere I could never have known about.

Lord Krishna gives meditation techniques to his disciples. They are utterly private and confidential, so I cannot tell you what they are. But I try to practise those techniques. Through practice, it's possible to really go into your heart and begin to reach God.

Since that special moment, I've had a high regard for my master, my guru.

NARNARAYAM P

FACT-FINDER

Meditation
For Hindus, meditating means emptying the mind of worldly thoughts in order to concentrate on God.

Disciples
Pupils or followers of someone's (here, Krishna's) teachings.

Guru
Spiritual teacher.

A special moment was when we bought this temple in 1970. I was one of the founders of the temple.

Back in the late sixties, it was hard for most of us to afford even a small house. So when we bought this temple, which is a large building, it was a great achievement for the community. All the more of an achievement bearing in mind how comparatively small the community was then.

RAMANBHAI

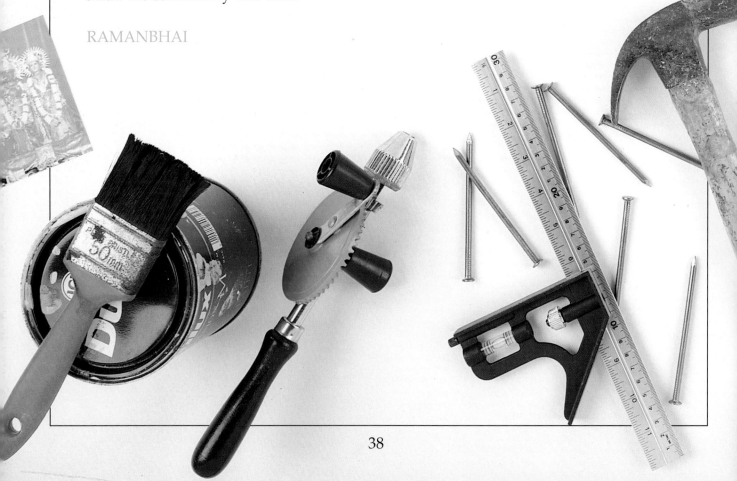

WORDS THAT MEAN A LOT TO ME

I find the Mahabharata and the Gita interesting. There's a bit where Kunti asks for unhappiness so she can get closer to God. When you're happy, you sometimes forget God. But when you're sad, you go to God and say, 'God, I've got this problem. Please help me.'

I don't know many people who'd ask for unhappiness, though. I don't think I'd ever ask for unhappiness. I'd probably ask for something nice. So about Kunti I thought, 'That's one person who really wants to get closer to God.'

Then there are all those prayers taken from the Gita. There's a prayer for eating, for instance. You say it before you eat. Actually, I don't say it myself. I want to learn the whole meaning of it first.

DEENA

FACT-FINDER

Mahabharata • Gita • Kunti

Kunti was the mother of Arjuna, one of the five sons of Pandu who feature in the Hindu sacred book called the Mahabharata, the 'Great Story of the Bharatas'. The Mahabharata is about rivalries in the Bharata dynasty for control of India's 'middle region' which eventually lead to an eighteen-day war.

On the eve of the first battle in this war, Arjuna's charioteer reveals himself as the god Krishna. Krishna sings the Bhagavad Gita ('Song of the Lord', part of the Mahabharata), convincing Arjuna of his duty to fight.

During the war, Arjuna kills his arch-rival Karna. Kunti then reveals that Karna was her son, born secretly when she was a young woman and left on the banks of the Yamuna river. Arjuna realizes he has killed his half-brother, and this news makes his victory bitter.

I have one short prayer I like and often use. It's a prayer for happiness in the world. There should be peace in the whole universe: in the stars, sun, planets, minerals, plants, animals and all human beings.

Another prayer is one I used when I was a student at school:

O God, let me, the student, and my teacher work in harmony;
Let us not be envious of each other;
Help us to work together to get knowledge,
And let that knowledge be bright and glorious
That we glorify each other.

Then there's this famous mantra:

O God, lead me from untruth to truth;
Lead me from darkness to light;
Lead me from mortality to immortality.
OM, shanti, shanti, shanti.

Our main scripture, the Vedas – 'veda' means 'knowledge' – reveals the quality of God through his creation. God creates a world in his image, just like a parent. Parents want their children to be like them or better than them.

'CM'

FACT-FINDER

Mantra
Sacred words repeated or chanted during prayer, worship or to aid meditation.

OM
Sacred syllable representing God used frequently in Hindu worship.

Shanti
Peace or tranquillity.

Words that are special to me are in the Gayatri Mantra. It's known throughout the Hindu world. Hindus say it frequently. The Gayatri Mantra comes from the Vedas. In Sanskrit it sounds like this:

OM bhur, bhuvah, swaha tat savitur varenyam bhargo devasya dhimahi, dhiyoyonah prachodavat.

It translates into English as:

O God, creator of the universe, who is everywhere and sustains everything, let our meditation be on your divine light and may that light illuminate our minds.

This mantra purifies the soul and concentrates the mind. We use it to pray for all people as well as for ourselves.

NARNARAYAM P

FACT-FINDER

Mantra · OM
See opposite.

Vedas
The oldest group of Hindu sacred books. Literally, 'veda' means 'knowledge'.

Sanskrit
Ancient language in which the Vedas and the other main Hindu sacred books are written.

Soul
Innermost part of a person, also called 'atman' by Hindus. The part that Hindus believe survives when the body dies.

H indu philosophy's very hard for people to grasp. I taught Hindu philosophy at school, and talking about philosophic principles can be very boring, so I would explain them through stories.

Hindu scripture uses stories a great deal. There are two classic books I like. One is the Panchatantra, the other is the Hitopadesa. The teacher tells a story to the children, then a lesson follows. It gets ideas across very quickly and it's fun. Those are words that mean a lot to me.

ASHOK

T he words which mean a lot to me are in the aarti. These are the words we use to offer our prayers here, at ten o'clock in the morning and seven o'clock in the evening. They all have equal significance.

What means more besides prayer is the knowledge, the Vedas. Now that is religion. Knowledge is what Hinduism is about, basically: OM, creation, everything follows knowledge, not a particular person. OK, there are the ideals, such as the gods Rama and Krishna, which we worship. But it's the knowledge which comes from them, that's what means a lot.

RAMESH B

FACT-FINDER

Hindu philosophy
The ideas, principles and reasoning on which Hinduism is based.

Panchatantra
Five (pancha) books (tantra) of tales dating from the sixth century C.E., based mostly on animals, birds and fish who behave like humans. Each tale is followed by a moral in verse and many are ingeniously linked.

Hitopadesa
See page 46.

Aarti
Act of worship where prayers are said or sung and a flame is circled in front of the image of a god or goddess.

Vedas
The oldest group of Hindu sacred books. Literally, 'veda' means 'knowledge'.

OM
Sacred syllable representing God used frequently in Hindu worship.

The prayer which I like most of all is the Brahmasabanta. (This word means 'relationship with God'.) In the prayer, the soul, a human being's soul, is praying to God:

It has been thousands of years that I have been separated from you. Now I would like to become one with you. And the joy that I will get to be with you will be infinite. O God, I the soul pray to you and bow to your feet. My body, all my senses, my life and heart, my duties – that is, husband or wife, home, children, family, wealth – this life and past life, everything is offered to you. O God, I am yours. O God, I am your humble servant.

I say that every morning. It's my choice. In Hinduism, there's no compulsion to pray this prayer or that prayer. You can pray at any time. You can pray however many times you want. There's no hard-and-fast rule.

So this prayer is special to me. In my mother's family, we used it a lot. That's how I learnt it. I was really interested in prayers as a child. I can still remember so many of the prayers my mother used to say in the morning. Now my own daughter knows them off by heart, too. She can't read them, but she can say them.

We have a small shrine at home. In our family, we believe in sanatan dharma – that means 'universal duty'. We believe in all the gods, not just in one, like Krishna or Rama. So we've got many portraits in our shrine. We try to light the lamp to them all.

ILLA

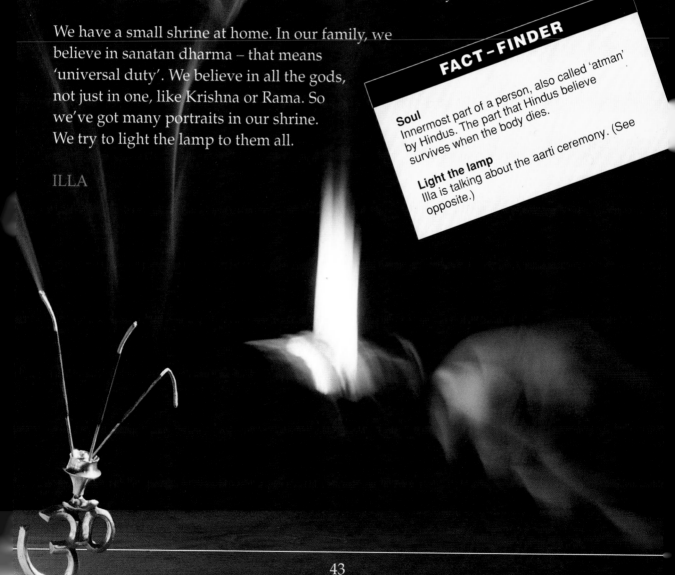

FACT-FINDER

Soul
Innermost part of a person, also called 'atman' by Hindus. The part that Hindus believe survives when the body dies.

Light the lamp
Illa is talking about the aarti ceremony. (See opposite.)

THINGS I FIND CHALLENGING

C hallenging is the amount of time you get to spare for your religion and your prayers here in Britain. You've got to try to find the time, but it's a challenge. Some Hindus are still facing up to it.

Here in Leicester there are a lot of Hindu families living together in one city, so it's not a matter of being in an unsympathetic community. It's more the pressure of a Western lifestyle.

We do try to compensate. For the children, we provide books, videos and audio-cassettes. And there's the temple itself. We're doing a lot here through work in the mother tongue – cultural programmes, support for Hindu families.

RAMANBHAI

W orking here at this temple is very challenging. A lot of people come to this temple and there's a range of different ideas and thinking. The whole time we're here, people come up to us with religious questions because we're Brahmin. And we have to answer them. That can often be challenging.

NARNARAYAM P

FACT-FINDER

Mother tongue
Ramanbhai means the Indian language the families spoke before they came to Britain. (See also page 11.)

Brahmin
Member of the priestly caste, the highest of the four main castes (groups) to which Hindus belong. (See also pages 14 and 16.)

I n this country, a big challenge is finding the time for your religious duties, especially when you're a housewife and you go to work and you look after the children.

You need a lot of patience. Especially with the children – how you talk to them, how you explain things to them. It's quite difficult when your children are growing up in a Western culture. They go out, mix with other children at school. Sometimes there can be a tension. It's in communication, really.

NIRU B

F inding time for everything is challenging. I've got so many things on. I've got the temple. I've got the school governor's role, in which I'm very active. I'm job seeking. I coach badminton. I'm trying hard to keep everything together. The family helps.

RAMESH B

Those who do hard work find that the result is always good. So I've always liked challenge and I've never been concerned about the future.

I can do anything with hard work. There's a moral from the Hitopadesa. The teacher says to his students: 'Always work hard. If you think you'd like to be a doctor or an engineer, you won't achieve anything just by thinking. You have to work.' Then he gives an example: 'Even though the lion's the king of the forest, his stomach won't fill on its own.'

When I went to the interview for my teaching job in India, I let God give me confidence and they selected me. When I applied to be a priest in Birmingham, I was corresponding from India with the Hindu temple committee. That didn't bother me. I got the job. There was a lot of competition for this post in Leicester, because this is an important temple. But if you're doing good things, God is behind you. God will help you and make sure your good work succeeds.

ASHOK

FACT-FINDER

Hitopadesa
Literally, 'Instruction in What Is Necessary'. This collection of stories is about an ideal society of animals who show how their talents, however small, can protect them against the ravages of stronger animals if used properly.

Twenty-five of the stories come from the Panchatantra (see page 42). The Hitopadesa has crossed continents and cultures in hundreds of translations, which include a Hebrew version with Jewish characters and an Arabic version with Muslim characters.

Guru
Spiritual teacher.

There is no challenge. If you believe, there is no challenge. Religion removes imbalance. Life goes easily. So I'm happy. All through my life I've been happy.

PRABHULAL

I'm always happy. Nothing troubles me. My master, my guru, has taught me to love other people. If you give love, love will come back to you. Wherever you are, give love and you'll not get hatred in return. Try to love. Give love and you'll get love.

DHANLAXMI P

There's a generation gap between older and younger Hindus in Britain, partly because some parents aren't able to pass on their culture and religion properly to their children. It's a language problem.

Youngsters come under Western influences at school, which makes them more independent. I'm not saying that's wrong. I don't see any reason why Indian culture and Hindu religion shouldn't go hand in hand with other ideas. They aren't necessarily opposites. But if parents aren't educating their children in the religion or the culture, then how can these things survive?

For instance, some Hindu children are confused about Hanuman and Ganesha. They see them as just a monkey god and an elephant god. Their parents tell them the Ramayana is just a story. But that's wrong. These are deities, forms of God. Hanuman is clever, strong and resourceful. He found Sita. Ganesha is sensitive, well read and knowledgeable. Their appearance is a disguise. The demon-king thought they were just animals of no significance. He thought he could kill them. He was wrong, too.

'CM'

FACT-FINDER

Ramayana • Sita • Demon-king
The Ramayana is one of the main Hindu sacred books. It tells the story of the god Rama, including how Hanuman and Ganesha helped him to rescue his wife Sita from the demon-king Ravana.

INDEX

Page numbers in **bold** type show where words or phrases are explained in FACT-FINDERS